RECONCILIATION SERVICES

Donal Neary SJ

Reconciliation Services

the columba press

First published in 2004 by
the columba press
55A Spruce Avenue, Stillorgan Industrial Park, Blackrock, Co Dublin

Cover by Bill Bolger
Origination by The Columba Press
Printed in Ireland by Colour Books Ltd, Dublin

ISBN 1 85607 431 5

Acknowledgements
The author gratefully acknowledges the permission of Linda Quigley to use Youth 3 from *Community of Love,* Veritas 2003.

Copyright © 2004, Donal Neary SJ

Contents

Introduction	6
Advent 1	9
Advent 2	14
Lent	18
For Schools: Lent	24
After Easter	28
Parish 1	33
Parish 2	38
Parish 3	42
Youth 1	48
Youth 2	52
Youth 3	58
On Retreat	62
For General Use	67
For Married Couples	73

Introduction

Reconciliation Services presents material for liturgies in a variety of settings. While each service is complete in itself, they will best be used with careful selection and adaptation, and even combinations of material from more than one service to suit the needs of various places and congregations.

Prayers, scripture and other readings, examination of life, silence, visuals and short rituals or activities are presented in each service. None should be used without some reservations: linking the material and the congregation envisaged is essential. The mood of a service may speak as much as words; thus the emphasis on visuals and symbols, and an encouragement to planned and sensitive use of lighting, music, candles and décor.

Scripture
A fresh variety of scripture has been selected; while the old stories and passages are suggested, others are also indicated with a reason for choosing them. Other stories from the life of Jesus or his teachings can be used. The homilist should pray through them so that the message is fresh and rooted in prayer. The forgiveness of Jesus is the theme of each service, with the title being a sub-theme.

Examination of Life
Lengthy lists of sins are avoided. An attempt has been made in the services to put the reflection on life and examination of life into a prayer for mercy, indicating areas of mercy which are relevant. Thus avoided are lists based on the ten commandments, or the seven deadly sins or the explanation of love in 1 Corinthians 13. The sacrament is meant to invite us into God's mercy more than into a list of what might have gone wrong in people's lives. Let's remember also that most people coming to the sacrament generally know what they want to confess. A teaching about sin is for another occasion, and maybe more relevant to those who do not come to the services of reconciliation. The focus of the sacrament is the personal relationship with Jesus within the community.

INTRODUCTION

Visuals
A penance service depends on more than words. The appearance of the sanctuary, the lighting in the church, what people can see, and hear and smell, are more important than many words.

An icon may be enthroned at the beginning of a service. If this is done, the icon should be big enough to be seen from the back of the church, bright enough also, either the icon itself or the lighting on it. An icon may be incensed, as may a crucifix or the paschal candle. We refrain from incensing other pictures, photos and candles.

The icon recalls either the season of the year or the theme of repentance. An icon or picture should speak of itself and not require much explanation.

The Homily
There does not have to be a homily! Sometimes notes are given, and the emphasis at the Reconciliation Service is to speak to the heart and move the whole person to sorrow, repentance, mercy and joy. It may be a good opportunity to invite a non-ordained man or woman to give a homily. Since the main part of the service is yet to come, any homily should be brief, moving towards conversion rather than knowledge. Explanation and encouragement rather than exhortation best moves the heart.

An Activity
Placing a candle in the sanctuary, placing a withered leaf as a sign of our deadness, a stone for our burdens – all these and other activities are suggested. They are not always limited to use in the particular service indicated, and can be used any time. People remember often more what they do than what they hear; many people have said that their activity at this point of the service has taught them a lot about the meaning of the sacrament.

Instructions should be clear and simple, as should the activity. People are invited to take part, not in any way co-erced. We may avoid very complicated rituals, remembering that lighting may be dimmed at this time. Instructions should also take account of impaired hearing and may need repetition.

If oil is used, people like to be reminded that this is not the sacrament of the sick; of if bread is used at any time, to be reminded that it is not holy communion.

The activity can take the longest to prepare. For example if we are using stone, someone has to collect them, clean them and have them there in time. But we never underestimate the prayerful and instructional value of the activity.

At a time when the sacrament of reconciliation causes confusion or boredom, the communal celebration, when prepared well, can be a mighty source of prayer and of the grace of God, who in Jesus Christ offers forgiveness, compassion, courage and strength to the all of us at our weakest.

Donal Neary SJ

ADVENT 1

On the Journey

1. This service of reconciliation is suitable for general use in Advent.
2. Necessary for the Service: Candles, decoration, posters etc for the central place or places of the ceremony. A visual of a pathway, if the service is in a small area. This can be made of sand or leaves on brown paper, suggesting the theme of Journey, or a basket to receive the names. Pencil and small pieces of paper for writing names. Scented oil for the anointing.
3. The selection of hymns depends on the repertoire of the congregation.

HYMN

INTRODUCTION
Welcome to our Advent celebration of reconciliation. The journey of God is a journey inviting us to reconciliation – to deepen our relationship with God, and with each other in Jesus Christ.
We recall this journey, and know we need the forgiveness and strength of God on our journey.

PRAYER
God of goodness and kindness,
you come to us in forgiveness and in our need for fullness in our lives.
We are men and women on the journey.
Help us, young and old, make this journey
in faith and in community,
in hope and in reconciliation.
Open us now to how good your world could be,
and how much we need to bring what is important to you
and your Son, Jesus,
into our world which needs you.
We make this prayer through Christ our Lord. **Amen.**

RECONCILIATION SERVICES

CALL TO REPENTANCE:
The call to repentance is from a God of faithfulness and mercy.

Who is a God like you, pardoning iniquity
and passing over the transgression
of the remnant of your possession?
He does not retain his anger for ever
because he delights in showing clemency.
He will again have compassion upon us,
he will tread our iniquities under foot.
You will cast all our sins
into the depths of the sea.
You will show faithfulness to Jacob
and steadfast love to Abraham,
as you have sworn to our ancestors
from the days of old.
(Micah 7:18-20)

GOSPEL:
We wait because all is not yet complete. Our world and our lives are incomplete; the way to full life is the way of God in Jesus. Our reading recalls the emptiness we sometimes experience in our waiting.
Waiting: Mary's waiting was active – in the sense that she went to her community and her cousin Elizabeth for help and support in her time of waiting. In the community of the church we wait for God's coming into our lives. It is a waiting in faith and in prayer, as is all waiting for the love of God.

In those days Mary set out and went with haste to a Judean town in the hill country, where she entered the house of Zechariah and greeted Elizabeth. When Elizabeth heard Mary's greeting, the child leaped in her womb. And Elizabeth was filled with the Holy Spirit and exclaimed with a loud cry, 'Blessed are you among women, and blessed is the fruit of your womb, And why has this happened to me, that the mother of my Lord comes to me? For as soon as I heard the sound of your greeting, the child in my womb leaped for joy.

ADVENT I

And blessed is she who believed that there would be a fulfillment of what was spoken to her from the Lord.'
(Luke 1:39-45)

PRAYER FOR MERCY:
Let us pray with confidence for the mercy of God:

For our impatience with others on our journey of life, **Lord have mercy.**
For our intolerance of the differences of others, **Lord have mercy.**
For our neglect of God in prayer, **Lord have mercy.**
For blindness to the needs of the poor, **Lord have mercy.**
For unwillingness to try to forgive, **Lord have mercy.**
For greed in our use of wealth, sexuality and comforts, **Lord have mercy.**
For forgetting to say the helpful word or do the helpful deed, **Lord have mercy.**
For being closed to the love of God, **Lord have mercy.**

May the Lord who forgives us our sins, heal our worries and anxieties, and bring us closer each day into his love.

RITUAL:
People are invited to write their name on a piece of paper, and place it on a pathway devised in the sanctuary, or into a basket. Our name sums up who we are, the good hopes of our lives, the sins, faults and failings.
This may be followed by individual confession, and on their return people are offered the anointing with oil to strengthen them on their journey.

During confession there may be music or hymns.

PRAYER OF THANKS AND PRAISE:
Mary's Magnificat is her thanks to God for all he has done for her. We make it our own, thanking him for forgiveness. We pray the Magnificat together:

RECONCILIATION SERVICES

And Mary said, 'My soul magnifies the Lord,
and my spirit rejoices in God my Saviour,
for he has looked with favour on the lowliness of his servant.
Surely, from now on all generations will call me blessed;
for the Mighty One has done great things for me,
and holy is his name.
His mercy is for those who fear him
from generation to generation.
He has shown strength with his arm,
he has scattered the proud in the thoughts of their hearts.
He has brought down the powerful from their thrones,
and lifted up the lowly;
he has filled the hungry with good things,
and sent the rich away empty.
He has helped his servant Israel,
in remembrance of his mercy,
according to the promise he made to our ancestors,
to Abraham and to his descendants for ever.'
And Mary remained with her about three months, and then returned to her home.
(Luke 1:46-56)

REFLECTION
We are blessed to believe in God:
Blessed, like Mary, to believe that God fulfils promises:
our baptism was his promise to love us all the days of our life,
our receiving the bread of life is his promise to nourish us on life's journey.

On our pilgrim way
we need to receive the cool water of forgiveness,
and to stand on the strong rock of faithfulness.
We thank God for love that never ends,
that is always near, especially when we are at our weakest.

We thank God for companions on the journey,
as Mary thanked God for Elizabeth,

ADVENT I

and Elizabeth for Mary at the time
of new life, new birth, old fears.
We are blessed to believe that all God promises us
is not just around the corner,
but beside us, here and now.

Let us pray:
Journey with us, God of our beginning and our end;
journey with us, God of our youth and old age;
journey with us, God of birth, death and resurrection.
May we welcome you as you journey to our world this time of year;
may you welcome us always in forgiveness and love
as we journey through life with you.
We make this prayer through Christ our Lord. **Amen.**

BLESSING
May the God of all times and places bless us with every good gift;
may the God of all peoples and races bless us with every joy;
and may the God of heaven and earth, Father, Son and Holy Spirit,
bless us and all dear to us, now and forever. **Amen.**

FINAL HYMN

ADVENT 2

Waiting in Hope

1. This service of reconciliation is suited for general use.
2. Necessary for the Service: Candles, decoration, posters etc for the central place or places of the ceremony. Calendars.
3. The selection of hymns depends on the repertoire of the congregation.

HYMN

In Advent we spend some time looking back on the year, and our lives. Christmas reminds us of other times, good and bad. God's people often look back and see how God loved them always. This helps us go forward in new faith. At Christmas we are aware of the compassion of God. God looks for us to save us, forgive us, bring us peace.

SETTING THE SCENE:
An invitation from the Lord:

You who fear the Lord, wait for his mercy;
do not stray, or else you may fall.
You who fear the Lord, trust in him,
and your reward will not be lost.
You who fear the Lord, hope for good things,
for lasting joy and mercy.
Consider the generations of old and see:
has anyone trusted in the Lord and been disappointed?
Or has anyone persevered in the fear of the Lord
and been forsaken?
Or has anyone called upon him and been neglected?
For the Lord is compassionate and merciful;
he forgives sins and saves in time of distress.
(Sirach 2:7-11.)

ADVENT II

PRAYER:

Lord, into your hands we place our past,
its joys and sorrows, success and failures, good times and bad.
Help us to see that you were always with us,
watching over us and protecting us,
loving us even when we were unfaithful or doing wrong.
We wait now in certainty of your mercy, for you are the God of love.
Be with us as we wait, be with us as we pray, be with us always in love,
through Jesus Christ our Lord, Amen.

FIRST READING:

A Reading from the Prophet Micah

Who is a God like you, pardoning iniquity
and passing over the transgression
of the remnant of your possession?
He does not retain his anger for ever
because he delights in showing clemency.
He will again have compassion upon us,
he will tread our iniquities under foot.
You will cast all our sins
into the depths of the sea.
You will show faithfulness to Jacob
and steadfast love to Abraham,
as you have sworn to our ancestors
from the days of old.
(Micah 7:18-20)

GOSPEL:

The prayer of Zechariah – the Benedictus – is a prayer about healing, forgiveness and welcome to the child of peace. As God promised through many prophets, now he is on his way among us. Many will announce him, including John the Baptist. His father makes this prayer for John at his birth.

RECONCILIATION SERVICES

Blessed be the Lord God of Israel,
for he has looked favourably on his people and redeemed them,
and has raised up a mighty saviour for us
in the house of his servant David,
as he spoke through the mouth of his holy prophets from of old,
that we should be saved from our enemies,
and from the hand of all who hate us.
Thus he has shown the mercy promised to our ancestors,
and has redeemed his holy covenant,
the oath that he swore to our father Abraham,
to grant us that we, being rescued from the hand of our enemies,
might serve him without fear,
in holiness and righteousness before him all our days.
And you, child, will be called the prophet of the Most High;
for you will go before the Lord to prepare his ways,
to give knowledge of salvation to his people
in the forgiveness of their sins.
By the tender mercy of our God,
the dawn from on high will break upon us,
to give light to those who sit in darkness and in the shadow of death,
to guide our feet into the way of peace.
(Luke 1:68-79.)

HOMILY NOTES:
The spouse who can see behind the weaknesses of his or her partner and forgive with an open heart: that is the merciful relationship. Mercy covers over the sin and the selfishness of the other, maybe knowing why another acts the way he or she does. That's the big name for God, he is a merciful God. His mercy is deeper than any other way he looks on us, even if he is angry with his people. The mother who gets annoyed when a child dirties the house but in the anger hugs the child – that's the merciful look and word. We become merciful people by knowing that we ourselves each of us is not perfect, that others have stories in their lives that explain them, and we become merciful to others when we know that God is merciful to them as he is to each of us.

ADVENT II

LITANY FOR FORGIVENESS:

AN ACTIVITY

Ask people to bring calendars they have at home, of any year. Place them on a central table with candles. They are reminders of God's love and care in the past. After confession, invite them to take a calendar home: a reminder of God's faithfulness. If there are not enough calendars, let people take a page of a calendar.

REFLECTION:

Carrier of God: Sacrament of Reconciliation

Each one of us is loved from 'before our birth'. As we follow the Lord Jesus in the days before his birth, we know that Mary is carrying one filled with the Spirit of God. We can be amazed at this fullness of God in a child, and then recall that each child is filled with the love of God from the first moment of conception. When a mother carries a child in her womb, and a father leads a child by the hand, they are carrying and leading the small body where God has made his home. Because of the gift of God, all of us belong in the stable of Bethlehem – we have in a sense been born there, since we are born in the love of God's Spirit, as were Jesus and John the Baptist. (From *Praying in Advent*, p 32.)

BLESSING

from Sirach 50:22-24

And now may God bless us all,
who everywhere works great wonders,
and who fosters our growth from birth,
and deals with us according to his great mercy.
May he give us gladness of heart,
and may there be peace in our days, as in the days of old.
May he entrust us to his mercy
and may he deliver us to freedom all the days of our lives.
May our good and gracious God bless us, now and always,
Father, Son and Holy Spirit. **Amen.**

FINAL HYMN

LENT

Invitation to Return

1. This service of reconciliation is for general use in Lent.
2. Necessary for the Service: Candles, decoration, posters etc for the central place or places of the ceremony. Cross, oil, pen/pencil and paper.
3. The selection of hymns depends on the repertoire of the congregation.

INTRODUCTION

Welcome to all who have come to be reconciled with God, and to celebrate this reconciliation. Lent is a season of returning; our service tonight takes as its theme 'returning to God'. We are coming back to a place where we belong – to the heart of God. We are returning to a person who wants us back, Jesus our friend. And we are drawn together in the Spirit of them both, God's Spirit of forgiveness.

PRAYER

Lord may I return
from selfishness to sensitivity,
from greed to generosity,
from coldness to caring,
from intolerance to compassion,
from isolation to community;

may I care for the earth, for friends and for the poor,
in memory and love of your care.

Allow me face the darkness of my past,
open me to the loving words of your gospel and of others,
give me healing, peace and forgiveness.

This is the prayer we all make, for ourselves and all here,
and all God's church,
in the name of Jesus who is Lord, now and forever. **Amen.**

CALL TO REPENTANCE:
Invitations to return to God for the forgiveness of our sins:

Turn back to the Lord and forsake your sins;
pray in his presence and lessen your offence.
Return to the most high and turn away from iniquity,
and hate intensely what he abhors.
How great is the mercy of the Lord,
and his forgiveness for those that return to him!
(Eccl 17:25-29.)

Or

Even now, says the Lord, return to me with all your heart,
With fasting, with weeping, with mourning.
Rend your hearts, not your clothing.
Return to the Lord your God, for he is gracious and merciful,
slow to anger, abounding in steadfast love,
and relents from punishing.
(Joel 2:12-14.)

HYMN

FIRST READING:
Our reading is an invitation to return to God even with sin and selfishness, and be refreshed and renewed in love.

The Lord says: 'Return, my people, to the Lord your God, for you have stumbled because of your sin. Take words with you and return to the Lord. Say to him, " Take away all guilt, accept that which is good and we will offer the fruit of our lips." I will heal their disloyalty, I will love them freely, for my anger has turned from them. They shall live again beneath my shadow, they shall flourish as a garden; they shall blossom like the vine, their fragrance shall be like the vine of Lebanon.' (*from Hosea 14:1-7).*

RECONCILIATION SERVICES

RESPONSORIAL

All *(sung or recited):* Come to me all you who are weary and overburdened and I will give you rest.

GOSPEL:

The Lord's joy in finding people who are lost, covering them with mercy and with love.

Or what woman, having ten silver coins, if she loses one coin, does not light a lamp and sweep the house and seek diligently until she finds it? And when she has found it, she calls together her friends and neighbours, saying, 'Rejoice with me, for I have found the coin which I had lost.' Just so, I tell you, there is joy before the angels of God over one sinner who repents.
(Luke 15: 6-11)

PRAYER FOR MERCY

Why do I not return?
Maybe because I feel the welcome would not be there, like water doesn't flow back up a hill, **Lord have mercy;**
maybe I know I'll sin again, like falling again over the same stone, **Lord have mercy;**
maybe I'm mean and ungenerous, and don't want to change any of my life, **Lord have mercy;**
maybe I am too heavily burdened with sin, shame and selfishness, **Lord have mercy;**
maybe I am just too full of discouragement and misery, **Lord have mercy.**

Lord Jesus, you are waiting, hand outstretched in care, **Lord have mercy.**
Lord Jesus, you are there, always patient, always compassionate, **Lord have mercy.**
Lord Jesus, you are waiting, risen in glory and in new life, **Lord have mercy.**

May God have mercy on us now and always,
and may we return to him confident of his forgiveness
now and forever. **Amen.**

LENT

HYMN

MOVEMENT OF RETURN:
To the Cross, to the Oil and back again.
The Cross is the principal visual for this service. People may place a list of their sins, their worries and anxieties on the cross; or their worries for others. As people give their piece of paper to be placed on the cross, they might be anointed with the oil of healing, of forgiveness and of strength. At this time is the opportunity for personal confession.

PRAYER OF ANOINTING:
May you receive the healing grace of Jesus Christ in your life, his strength and forgiveness all the days of your life.

Individual confession may be available at this time. Music may be played, hymns sung during the confession time. Reflections may also be read.

REFLECTIONS
One or more may be read during Confessions between hymns, or one before the final prayer.

There's a time and a place for everything,
for living and dying, resting and rising,
for work and for leisure, for speaking and listening,
there's a time for God and a time for people,
a time for confessing and a time for commitments;

and there's a time and a place for the forgiveness of God;
in the heart of God and in the love of God in Jesus,
that time is now, and that time is always.
There's never a time when God is not forgiving,

May the God of mercy, love, and of comfort,
hear our sorrow for the past,
hear our hopes for the future,
and give us now and always, love and forgiveness
and bring us to everlasting life. **Amen.**

RECONCILIATION SERVICES

Let us pray as Jesus taught us, for forgiveness:
Our Father …

We pray for peace and harmony in all of God's creation:
Lord Jesus Christ, you said to your apostles …
We offer each other a sign of peace.

Reflections:
The mother spending all day in the hospital with a sick child
while the others at home fare for themselves.
A father worrying over the son or daughter in trouble,
and the others wonder does he think of them –
there are times when the lost one or the sick one takes all our time.

The lost sheep is the one sought and searched for
and there's a risk that while the shepherd is away
the others will be lost or attacked,
and to all is the invitation to return.

There's a special place in the heart of Jesus for when we are lost;
and for the ones in society nobody cares for.
That's the mercy of God – never asking why but just loving.

That's forgiveness also – never again asking why but looking ahead.

The Lord is seeking you, searching for you, loving you this moment
to let you know that he forgives you, forgiven forever.

Or
The past can haunt.
We know the secrets that make us shudder –
people we have hurt and the memories cause guilt,
injustices we could have prevented,
and the bitterness and harshness which are part of life.

Everyone has a past, and can bring the past for healing.
The grace of God flows, reaches, touches into the past
So that the painful haunts of the past are healed,
and life is new, free and reconciled.

Our past is forgiven though not forgotten,
sins and failings can be stepping stones on the ladder of love,
and the Lord is glad that our faces turn always towards him,
and our steps turn in his direction.

FINAL PRAYER:
Lord of forgiveness and Lord of compassion,
we pray that we may be truly grateful for your forgiveness in our lives
and for the forgiveness of each other.
May all we do and say be in the spirit of forgiveness,
love and reconciliation.
We make this prayer through Christ our Lord. Amen.

BLESSING:
As we leave this place we pray the blessing of the holy anointing:
may you be blessed always with the peace of the Lord.

As we leave this place we pray the blessing of the journey:
may we find the Lord waiting for us wherever we go.

As we leave this place we pray the blessing of the Cross:
may the cross of Jesus be always the way to risen joy.
And may God bless us now and always,
Father, Son and holy Spirit. **Amen.**

HYMN

FOR SCHOOLS: LENT

Bread and Stone

1. This service of reconciliation is suitable for school use in Lent.
2. Necessary for the Service: Candles, decoration, posters etc for the central place or places of the ceremony. Large stone and some bread for the centre piece.
3. The selection of hymns depends on the repertoire of the congregation.

WELCOME AND HYMN:
We come to ask God for forgiveness and for strength in our lives. God loves us in our faults and failings, no matter what. We know he will give us this, so we can pray in confidence. All are welcome to take part in our prayer for forgiveness and our sacrament of reconciliation.

PRAYER:
We come before you, Father,
confident that you know us better than we know ourselves.
Help us to be honest during this hour,
so that we may come to a better understanding of ourselves
and our attitudes to you and to each other.
We make our prayer through Christ our Lord. **Amen.**

GOSPEL:
God wants to give us the Holy Spirit's gifts of love and forgiveness in our lives if only we ask.

A reading from the Gospel according to St Luke:
Jesus said to his disciples: 'Suppose one of you has a friend and you to him at midnight and say to him, "Friend, lend me three loaves of bread; for a friend of mine has arrived, and I have nothing to set before him." And he answers from within, "Do not bother me; the door has already been locked, and my children are with me in bed; I cannot get up and give you

anything"? I tell you, even though he will not get up and give him anything because he is his friend, at least because of his persistence he will rise and give him whatever he needs.

So I say to you, Ask, and it will be given you; seek, and you will find; knock, and the door will be opened for you. For every one who asks receives, and everyone who seeks finds, and for everyone who knocks the door will be opened.

Is there anyone among you, if your child asks for a fish, will give a snake- instead of a fish? Or if the child asks for an egg, will give a scorpion? If you then, who are evil, know how to give good gifts to your children, how much more will the heavenly Father give the Holy Spirit to those who ask him!'
(Luke 11:5-13.)

REFLECTION ON LIFE:
You are either bread or stone:
First Reader: You are either bread or stone.
Second Reader: Bread can be broken and shared with others.
First Reader: Stone is hard and cold.
Second Reader: When I accept to share what I have with others ... when I take the time to help someone in need ... I am bread for others.
First Reader: When I am selfish and think only of myself ... when all I am interested in is taking advantage of others ... when I am cold with those who could use my friendship ... I am stone for others.
Second Reader: Bread is good to eat and it gives life.
First Reader: When I respect others and treat them with kindness ... when I am a peacemaker where there is tension ... when I forgive those who have hurt me ... I am bread for them. I give them life.
Second Reader: When I put others down or I laugh at them ... when I gossip ... when I want revenge I am like stone. There is no life in me.
First Reader: With stones, you can break things.
Second Reader: When you use hard thoughts, hard words, hard actions with those around you and treat them as your enemies, you are like a stone thrown through a beautiful stained glass window, shattering the lives of those around you.
First Reader: Bread is soft and lets itself be eaten.

RECONCILIATION SERVICES

Second Reader: When I think well of others and help them see the goodness of God through me, I am like soft bread that feeds and gives strength.
First Reader: We have a choice … we can be stone for others, … we can be bread for them … which have you been lately? Which do you want to be?

PRAYER OF SORROW

O my God, I am sincerely sorry for the wrong things I have done. I ask for pardon and peace. Give me the strength and courage to try again; to live my life as you have shown me, like the way Jesus lived. Help me Lord in my efforts to live like a Christian. Finally Lord, give me happiness and joy in my life, and help me to show your love by the way that I live. Amen.

OUR FATHER

We pray with confidence to God as Jesus has taught us:
Our Father *(in traditional form or the following)*:

Our Father you are in us here on earth and holy is your name.
May your kingdom come in this land which is rich with good things.
Let us do your will standing up when others sit down
and raising our voices when others are silent.
You are giving us our daily bread in the song of the bird
and the miracle of life itself.
Forgive us for keeping silent when others are treated badly,
for not following our dreams and not sharing our gifts.
Do not let us fall into the temptation of shutting the door
because we are too cowardly to face the truth.
Deliver us from the fear of failure and help us to love
and make a place for you in our lives. **Amen.**

PRAYER

Loving Creator and Giver of everything that is good.
We have looked at our lives in the light of your mercy
and received your forgiveness in the blessing of Jesus our Brother.
Strengthen our resolve to renew our lives in this way in the coming months
so that we may develop as fully mature human beings,
in our relationships and friendships, with you and with each other.
We make our prayer through Christ our Lord. **Amen.**

FOR SCHOOLS: LENT

BLESSING

May the Father of mercy and forgiveness let you know he loves you;
May Jesus who died for the love of all of you let you know he loves you;
And may the Spirit of Father and Son, the God of peace, give you the courage and help you need to live in love. May God bless you now and always, Father, Son and holy Spirit. **Amen.**

Go in the peace and forgiveness of Christ.

HYMN

(With acknowledgement to Mary Gallagher, Chaplain, Coláiste Chiaráin, Leixlip, and RE News, Dublin Diocese.)

AFTER EASTER

Receive the Holy Spirit

1. This service of reconciliation is for a prayer/reflection day for Easter time.
2 Necessary for the Service: Candles, decoration, posters etc for the central place or places of the ceremony. Bread, rocks, sand.
3. Yhe selection of hymns depends on the repertoire of the congregation.

INTRODUCTION
As a centre piece, try to have something which captures the generosity of God, like a lavish display of flowers, a tree or plant vibrant with growth and colour, a tapestry of many colours with some intimation of resurrection, the scent of burning oil or incense, or a water fountain.

The centre piece may be adapted for each of the suggested gospels.

OPENING PRAYER
Good and gracious God of mercy,
you call us to repentance and to your mercy.
Give us honesty, humility and hope.
We ask this through the risen Jesus
who is our Lord now and forever. **Amen.**

CALL TO REPENTANCE
A call to be humble of heart.
Your proud heart has deceived you,
you that live in the cleft of the rock,
whose dwelling is in the heights.
You say in your heart,
'who will bring me down to the ground?'
Though you soar aloft like the eagle,
though your nest is set among the stars,
from there I will bring you down. *(Obadiah 1: 3-4)*

AFTER EASTER

READINGS:
The generosity of God's mercy
We do not think like God; neither do we forgive like God.

Seek the Lord while he may be found,
call upon him while he is near;
let the wicked forsake his way,
and the unrighteous their thoughts;
let them return to the Lord, that he may have mercy on them,
and to our God, for he will abundantly pardon.
For my thoughts are not your thoughts,
neither are your ways my ways, says the Lord.
For as the heavens are higher than the earth,
so are my ways higher than your ways
and my thoughts than your thoughts.
(Isaiah 55:6-9.)

Response: The Lord is kind and full of compassion

The Lord is merciful and gracious,
slow to anger and abounding in steadfast love.
He will not always chide,
nor will he keep his anger for ever.

He does not deal with us according to our sins,
nor requite us according to our iniquities.
For as the heavens are high above the earth,
so great is his steadfast love toward those who fear him;
as far as the east is from the west,
so far does he remove our transgressions from us.

As a father pities his children,
so the Lord pities those who fear him.
For he knows our frame;
he remembers that we are dust.

RECONCILIATION SERVICES

GOSPEL 1

This breakfast was a meal of reconciliation and forgiveness. Maybe this was the first time some of them had met since the death of Jesus; maybe the first time he had met some of them. Forgiveness would be needed, and was in the air. They needed the forgiveness of Jesus after their denials and neglect of him, and they had run away. And they needed the forgiveness of each other for the ways they had not supported each other's faith and convictions about Jesus. The bread offered was the forgiveness of God, offered each time we receive the Eucharist.
Think of images of that – the image of bread from different parts of the world in a centre piece (soda bread, nan bread, black bread, croissants …); or an image of bread and fish; or rock and sand onto which people may put their stone of sin.

After these things Jesus showed himself again to the disciples by the Sea of Tiberias; and he showed himself in this way.
Gathered together were Simon Peter, Thomas called the Twin, Nathanael of Cana in Galilee, the sons of Zebedee, and two others of his disciples. Simon Peter said to them, 'I am going fishing.' They said to him, 'We will go with you.' They went out and got into the boat, but that night they caught nothing.
Just after daybreak, Jesus stood on the beach; but the disciples did not know that it was Jesus. Jesus said to them, 'Children, you have no fish, have you?' They answered him, 'No.' He said to them, 'Cast the net to the right side of the boat, and you will find some.' So they cast it, and now they were not able to haul it in, because there were so many fish. That disciple whom Jesus loved said to Peter, 'It is the Lord!' When Simon Peter heard that it was the Lord, he put on some clothes, for he was naked, and jumped into the sea. But the other disciples came in the boat, dragging the net full of fish, for they were not far from the land, but about a hundred yards off.
When they had gone ashore, they saw a charcoal fire there, with fish on it, and bread. Jesus said to them, 'Bring some of the fish that you have just caught.' So Simon Peter went aboard and hauled the net ashore, full of large fish, a hundred and fifty-three of them; and though there were so many, the net was not torn. Jesus said to them, 'Come and have breakfast.' Now none of the disciples dared to ask him, 'Who are you?' because they

AFTER EASTER

knew it was the Lord. Jesus came and took the bread and gave it to them, and did the same with the fish.
(John 21:1-13.)

Or

GOSPEL 2
A gift was offered which was needed, and this was the gift of the risen Lord. He breathed forgiveness on them, and they knew that the breath of God recreated them, as later the fire of the Spirit would energise them. They needed personal forgiveness after the death of Christ, and this new life of Jesus offered just that.
Think of images of breath and fire, which are the life and the energy of the Spirit.

When it was evening on that day, the first day of the week, and the doors of the house where the disciples had me were locked for fear of the Jews, Jesus came and stood among them and said, 'Peace be with you.' After he said this, he showed them his hands and his side. Then the disciples rejoiced when they saw the Lord. Jesus said to them again, 'Peace be with you. As the Father has sent me, so I send you.' When he had said this, he breathed on them, and said to them, 'Receive the Holy Spirit. If you forgive the sins of any, they are forgiven; if you retain the sins of any, they are retained.'
(John 20:19-23.)

LITANY OF FORGIVENESS
We confess our failures to give what we can in our lives:

for failures in generosity, **Lord have mercy,**
for failures in tolerance of others, **Lord have mercy,**
for failures to do our best in work, **Lord have mercy,**
for failures to do our best in study, **Lord have mercy,**
for failures to rejoice in the good fortunes of others, **Lord have mercy.**

Make us generous in sharing our talents and what we have, **Lord have mercy,**

RECONCILIATION SERVICES

Make us tolerant of other sin all we think and say, **Lord have mercy,**
Bless our efforts in work and study, **Lord have mercy,**
Bless us in all we do, say and think, **Lord have mercy,**
Bless us in our joy in the goodness of others, **Lord have mercy.**

During confessions, play music reminiscent of Easter (e.g. Taizé Alleluias).

On way back people collect a small fruit … something which reminds us of the new life of Easter – maybe a grape, a strawberry if these are in season … something which costs little. This fruit can be brought home.

REFLECTION
Think of a wide expanse of sand,
A beach you like to walk on or look over.
Stretching right and left of you, ahead and behind.
This is spaciousness, colour, peace.
It is the generosity of God's creation.
Be grateful for spaciousness and generosity.
And his mercy is like that:
The heart of God is big, generous, compassionate.
Wide enough for the biggest sinner's shelter,
and for peace for deepest worries.
In this love Jesus lived,
the one whose generosity rewards all efforts
to live in love, forgiveness and reconciliation.

BLESSING
May we know in our hearts the compassion of Jesus,
and may we know in our minds the truth of his forgiveness.

May we know the peace of Christ which is beyond all understanding in our hearts, minds and bodies.

May God's forgiveness to ourselves be noticed in our forgiveness of each other. May the Father of life, the Son of forgiveness and the Spirit of reconciliation bless us now and always. **Amen.**

HYMN

PARISH 1

The Call to Deeper Love

1. This service of reconciliation is for general parish use.
2. Necessary for the Service: Candles, decoration, posters etc for the central place or places of the ceremony. Salt and a bowl of water.
3. The selection of hymns depends on the repertoire of the congregation.

INTRODUCTION:
Jesus wants us to be better people, kinder, more loving, more fully alive. As simple as that. It happens by his grace more than our own efforts. It happens when we know we are deeply loved. Forgiveness makes us better people, more whole, more human. He takes us as we are and leads us to what we might become.

PRAYER
God of mercy and compassion, we your people, of many ages and backgrounds, faith and unbelief, return to you, for you have invited us in your love. Gather the fragments of our love, hope, sin and failures, so that we may rejoice always in who we are and in your love for us. Grant this through Christ our Lord. **Amen.**

CALL OF THE LORD TO REPENTANCE:
You shall know that I am in the midst of my people,
and that I the Lord, am your God, and there is no other.
(Joel 2:27.)

SCRIPTURE:
This service hinges on two gospel stories, one a challenge to forgive, and the other a story of strength to know we are forgiven, and that we can find deep freedom in forgiving.

RECONCILIATION SERVICES

GOSPEL:
How often must I forgive my brother?

Then Peter came up and said to him, 'Lord, if another member of the church sins against me, how often should I forgive? As many as seven times?' Jesus said to him, 'Not seven times, but, I tell you, seventy-seven times.'
'For this reason the kingdom of heaven may be compared to a king who wished to settle accounts with his slaves. When he began the reckoning, one who owed him ten thousand talents was brought to him; and, as he could not pay, his lord ordered him to be sold, together with his wife and children and all his possessions, and payment to be made. So the slave fell on his knees before him, saying, 'Have patience with me, and I will pay you everything.' And out of pity for him the lord of that slave released him and forgave him the debt. But that same slave, as he went out, came upon one of his fellow slaves who owed him a hundred denarii; and seizing him by the throat he said, 'Pay what you owe.' Then his fellow slave fell down and pleaded with him, 'Have patience with me, and I will pay you.' But he refused; then he went and threw him into prison until he would pay the debt. When his fellow slaves saw what had happened, they were greatly distressed, and they went and reported to their lord all that had taken place. Then his lord summoned him and said to him, 'You wicked slave! I forgave you all that debt because you pleaded with me. Should not you have had mercy on your fellow slave, as I had mercy on you?' And in anger his lord delivered him to be tortured until he would pay his entire debt. So my heavenly Father will also do to every one of you, if you do not forgive your brother or sister from your heart.'
(Mt 18:21-35.)

Or
The man with the withered hand.

Again he entered the synagogue, and a man was there who had a withered hand. They watched him, to see whether he would cure him on the sabbath, so that they might accuse him. And he said to the man who had the withered hand, 'Come forward.' Then he said to them, 'Is it lawful to do

good or to do harm on the sabbath, to save life or to kill?' But they were silent. He looked around at them with anger; he was grieved at their hardness of heart and said to the man, 'Stretch out your hand.' He stretched it out, and his hand was restored. The Pharisees went out, and immediately conspired with the Herodians against him, how to destroy him.
(Mark 3:1-6.)

REFLECTION ON LIFE

We pause and remember our sins; ways we have hurt others and let ourselves down:
In how we talk about others; in how we use others for our own reputation, pleasure or prosperity;
In how we neglected to notice pain and tough times in the lives of those closest to us;
In using God's creation selfishly and failing to give thanks for the beauty of this world;
In all the ways we know we might have been better men and women,
I confess ...

PRAYER

May the good and gracious God, creator of everything in us, forgive us our sins, lead us to know how good we could be, and give us the help we need to follow the example of the Lord Jesus in our lives. We make this prayer through Christ our Lord. **Amen.**

ON THE WAY FOR THE SACRAMENT:

Take some salt, the seasoning for all we eat, and place it in the bowl of water: salt 'seasons' our baptism so that it is a promise for all time, will strengthen and keep fresh the love and forgiveness of God in our lives. Confession may follow.
On return from confession, place your hand in the water of life and make the sign of the cross with this water.

HYMN

RECONCILIATION SERVICES

REFLECTION:
The Withered Hand

He came with his hand all withered, by his side,
up his sleeve that nobody might see,
and anyway it would not move anywhere else for him.
They often called him names – 'where's your hand?'
Or 'the handyman',
and all he wanted was that nobody would ever say,
'Stand out here in the middle and let's see your hand.'

Like stand out in the middle and let's hear your stutter
or stand in the middle and let's hear your croaky singing voice
or stand in the middle and let's see the scar on your neck
stand out in the middle and we'll mock your family …
or call you names –
all that 'standing the middle witherdness' we hate to admit.

All that was out in the middle now
and the man was suffering.
But he looked up
and he knew the best man in the synagogue was on his side;
and the middle seemed a safe enough place to be
because Jesus had come out into the middle to be near him.

He never took his eyes off the one who asked him
and then, only then, could he stretch out his hand.
Strong, cured, without a touch,
with a searching look that both gave and demanded faith.
with only a look from the eye of compassion,
and the memory of the look lasts forever.

PRAYER FOR PEACE
from the Mass
Let us offer each other a sign of the peace of God.

PRAYER

We pray in the name of the Lord
of daybreak, noon, evening and night;
of light and darkness, light and shadow, light and dusk.
Christ at every beginning,
at every end.
Christ at the turn of every year, at the bend of every road.

Christ in dark's deep shadows, Christ in shades of death and sin,
Christ in all our country's history, in all the seasons of earth.

Christ in joy and sadness, heaviness and humour,
Christ in our fallings and our risings,
Christ in death, Christ in resurrection,
Saviour, Lord, Brother and Son of the Father, **Amen.**

BLESSING

The One who forms the mountains and creates the winds will bless you with gentleness.
The One who reveals his thoughts to mortals will bless you with wisdom.
The One who gives his Christ to the world will bless you with love.
May God bless you now and always, Father, Son and Holy Spirit. **Amen.**

HYMN.

PARISH 2

God of the Second Chance

1. This service of reconciliation is for general use.
2. Necessary for the Service: Candles, decoration, posters etc for the central place or places of the ceremony. Bread, bowls of water, shells.
3. The selection of hymns depends on the repertoire of the congregation.

INTRODUCTION

We are never forgotten by God, and he never gives up on us. We may give up on ourselves. He is the God of the Second Chance, the third and the umpteenth chance. The invitation this day is to return, even if we feel we are always returning.

PRAYER

Lord of mercy and of hope,
you are kind, you are gracious, you are compassionate.
We come to you at your invitation to be loved and forgiven.
Your heart is ever open to us, even when we fall again and again.
Give us faith in your kindness, your graciousness and your compassion.
You are our Lord and Brother, now and forever. **Amen.**

READING:

An invitation to return, always a word in the heart of God, hoping we may return to him.

Come, let us return to the Lord; for he has torn, that he may heal us; he has struck down, and he will bind us up. After two days he will revive us; on the third day he will raise us up, that we may live before him. Let us know, let us press on to know the Lord; his appearing is sure as the dawn; he will come to us like the showers, as the spring rains that water the earth. What shall I do with you, O Ephraim? What shall I do with you, O Judah? Your love is like a morning cloud, like the dew that goes early away.

Therefore I have hewn them by the prophets, I have slain them by the words of my mouth, and my judgement goes forth as the light.
For I desire steadfast love and not sacrifice, the knowledge of God, rather than burnt offerings.
(Hosea 6: 1-6.)

GOSPEL:

Jesus compares himself to the shepherd looking for the one who was lost. No blame that the sheep got lost, just the Lord Jesus goes to look for him, and wants his return.

Now the tax collectors and sinners were coming near to listen to him. And the Pharisees and the scribes were grumbling and saying, 'This fellow welcomes sinners and eats with them.'
So he told them this parable: 'Which one of you, having a hundred sheep and losing one of them, does not leave the ninety-nine in the wilderness, and go after the one that is lost until he finds it? And when he has found it, he lays it on his shoulders and rejoices. And when he comes home, he calls together his friends and neighbours, saying to them, 'Rejoice with me, for I have found my sheep that was lost.' Just so, I tell you, there will be more joy in heaven over one sinner who repents than over ninety-nine righteous persons who need no repentance.
(Luke 15: 1-7.)

EXAMINING OUR LIVES:

For our misuse and destruction of the resources of the earth, **Lord have mercy.**
For ways in which we have put our comfort above the needs of others, **Lord have mercy.**
For ways in which we have put our sexual needs above the needs of others, **Lord have mercy.**
For overindulgence in food and drink, **Lord have mercy.**
For neglecting to care for our health and well-being, **Lord have mercy.**
For ignoring the needs of the poor and the needy, **Lord have mercy.**
For ignoring the needs and sufferings of those closest to us, **Lord have mercy.**

RECONCILIATION SERVICES

For ignoring the inequality of our world, **Lord have mercy.**
For neglect of prayer and worship, **Lord have mercy.**
For bitter moments, judgements and thoughts, **Lord have mercy.**
For failing to be thankful for the good things of life, **Lord have mercy.**

We now pray together:
I confess ...

May our good and loving God have mercy on us, forgive us our sins, and bring us to everlasting life. **Amen.**

HYMN

A RITUAL
A table of bread is prepared, and onto this table each places a small purple ribbon, which is the sign of our sins and faults and failings, knowing that the bread of life is the bread of forgiveness. The bread should be of different kinds. Bread was a sign for Jesus of fellowship and the Eucharist was one among many meals he shared with people.
This may be followed by individual confession.

Bowls of water are prepared, and as people come back from the table or from confession, they wash their hands in the water of baptism. Shells may be placed on a table, which each person may take – reminder of the beach which was the place of meeting for Jesus and the disciples, and signs of eternity.

A BREAKFAST REFLECTION:
A new day and a new dawn,
new hopes, new optimism.

The dawn is refreshing and is certain;
breakfast renews energy and awakens.
God, always forgiving,
renews old hopes and shatters shame,
refreshes desires to love and scatters guilt,

calling always anew,
'Come with me, love with me, serve with me;
for God has called
and you are one,
one with me, one with all.
Come and have breakfast,
Come and be forgiven,
Come and be fed with the bread and love of life.'

PRAYER

Lord of mercy and love, we have allowed ourselves admit our need for you, and our need for forgiveness. We know you as always giving another chance. This is a moment of grace and hope for us as we know that. We are grateful for forgiveness and for strength, and pray now on each person here your blessing, through Christ our Lord. **Amen.**

FINAL BLESSING

May God who is father and mother to us bless us with compassion, compassion from him and for others;
May God who is Son and word bless us with forgiveness, forgiveness from him and for others;
May God who is Spirit bless us with freedom from guilt and from shame, and may these be the gifts of Father, Son and Holy Spirit;
May God bless us now and always, Father, Son and Holy Spirit. **Amen.**

HYMN.

PARISH 3

Forgiveness: The Golden String

1. This service of reconciliation is suitable for general parish use.
2. Necessary for the Service: Candles, decoration, posters etc for the central place or places of the ceremony. The paschal candle may be centrally placed and lit. Have ready small-cut pieces of golden wool or a golden coloured ribbon: they remind people of the love of God, like the golden string in life. Ensure there are enough for everyone, and have one or two lay people give them to people after they have gone to confession, or they can come up for the golden string if not going to confession then.
3 The selection of hymns depends on the repertoire of the congregation.

HYMN

WELCOME

A sincere welcome to all who have come this day/night to celebrate and ask for reconciliation with God. Reconciliation with God involves a willingness to forgive each other. A welcome especially to anyone who is here for the first time, or who feels a special burden of guilt or anxiety, and to those who may not have been to this sacrament for some time. We meet in the name of Jesus Christ, the one who offers peace and strength to all in living our Christian life.

INTRODUCTION

We gather around the candle of Easter, aware that forgiveness is a gift of the risen Lord.
The Lord now risen will never die again, and our sins now forgiven are never held to our account. We gather as the apostles did as the community of God's people, and offer in our prayer and in our relationships the forgiveness of God to each other.

READING
The call in this reading is to listen to the good desires and convictions of the heart of a follower of Jesus, and live by them.

See, I have set before you today life and prosperity, death and adversity. If you obey the commandments of the Lord your God that I am commanding you today, by loving the Lord your God, walking in his ways, and observing his commandments, decrees and his ordinances, then you shall live and become numerous, and the Lord your God will bless you in the land that you are entering to possess. But if your heart turns away, and you do not hear, but are led astray to bow down to other gods and serve them, I declare to you today that you shall perish; you shall not live long in the land that you are crossing the Jordan to enter and possess.
(Deuteronomy 30:15-18.)

Or
An invitation to return to God.

Return, O Israel, to the Lord your God,
for you have stumbled because of your iniquity.
Take words with you and return to the Lord;
say to him, 'Take away all guilt;
accept that which is good and we will offer the fruit of our lips.
Assyria shall not save us, we will not ride upon horses;
and we will say no more, 'Our God,' to the work of our hands.
In you the orphan finds mercy.

I will heal their disloyalty;
I will love them freely, for my anger has turned from them.
I will be like the dew to Israel; he shall blossom like the lily,
he shall strike root like the forest of Lebanon.
His shoots shall spread out; his beauty shall be like the olive tree,
and his fragrance like that of Lebanon.

They shall return and dwell beneath my shadow,
they shall flourish as a garden;

they shall blossom like the vine,
their fragrance shall be like the wine of Lebanon.

O Ephraim, what have I to do with idols?
It is I who answer and look after you.
I am like an evergreen cypress,
your faithfulness comes from me.
Those who are wise understand these things;
those who are discerning know them.
For the ways of the Lord are right,
and the upright walk in them,
but transgressors stumble in them.
(Hosea 14:1-9.)

HYMN

GOSPEL:
In the circle around Jesus is a woman who is ashamed of her sin. Somehow the care of Jesus accepts her and she can admit she is a sinner and in need of healing and mercy. We admit to each other that we are sinners.

Now there was a woman who had been suffering from haemorrhages for twelve years; and though she had spent all she had on physicians, no one could cure her. She came up behind him and touched the fringe of his clothes, and immediately her hemorrhage stopped. Then Jesus asked, 'Who touched me?' When all denied it, Peter said, 'Master, the crowds surround you and press in on you.' But Jesus said, 'Someone touched me; for I noticed that power had gone out from me.' When the woman saw that she could not remain hidden, she came trembling; and falling down before him, she declared in the presence of all the people why she had touched him, and how she had been immediately healed. He said to her, 'Daughter, your faith has made you well; go in peace.'
(Luke 8:43-48.)

EXAMINATION OF LIFE:
For neglect of friends, **Lord have mercy.**
For neglect of family, **Lord have mercy.**
For neglect of the poor, **Lord have mercy.**
For neglect of heath and body, **Lord have mercy.**
For neglect of the earth, **Lord have mercy.**
For neglect of spouse, **Lord have mercy.**
For neglect of God, **Lord have mercy.**
I confess …

May God the Father of all kindness and comfort forgive us our sins.
May God's Son, the Word of all understanding and tolerance look kindly on our faults; as he has forgiven us, may we forgive each other.
May the Spirit of God, of forgiveness and reconciliation, breathe peace and love on us all.
We ask this through Christ our Lord. **Amen.**

Together we pray some verses of the great psalm of sorrow, Psalm 51:
Response:
Have mercy on me, O God,
in your compassion and in your kindness blot out my sins.

Have mercy on me, O God,
according to your steadfast love;
according to your abundant mercy blot out my transgressions.

Wash me thoroughly from my iniquity,
and cleanse me from my sin!
For I know my transgressions,
and my sin is ever before me.

Fill me with joy and gladness;
let the bones which thou hast broken rejoice.
Hide your face from my sins,
and blot out all my iniquities.
Create in me a clean heart, O God,
and put a new and right spirit within me.

RECONCILIATION SERVICES

Cast me not away from your presence,
and take not your holy Spirit from me.

TIME FOR INDIVIDUAL CONFESSION

As people come back from the confession, as they pass by the paschal candle they pray their penance at the candle of the risen Lord. Then they take a golden string, a reminder of the golden string in life which is the love and forgiveness of God.

HYMN

REFLECTION:

Through all weakness in life runs the golden string of God's strength,
through all the sin, the golden string of his forgiveness,
through all hurt, the golden string of his healing love,
a golden string which has been part of the colour of life.

With a string of love he guides us through life,
a golden light in all life's darkness,
a golden echo in life's stridency.

Encircled with the golden string,
we journey with the confidence which is born of love,
the love of God from birth to death,
the love of others on life's path,
the love which forgives
and embraces the past, present and the future of every life.

FINAL BLESSING:

May God of our fathers and mothers
who called Abraham and Sarah to journey into the unknown
be with you on your journey of life.
May the God who guarded and blessed them,
protect you also and bless your journey.

May God's confidence support you
and may God's Spirit be with you;
and may God lead you always in his peace
and care lovingly for those we commend to his care;
God is with them, and we shall not fear.
As for ourselves,
may God's presence be our companion
so that blessing may come to us and to everyone we meet.
Blessed are you, Lord God,
your presence travels with your people.
Blessed are you now and forever. Amen.
(Adapted from *Jewish Prayer Book*.)

HYMN.

YOUTH 1

What You Do To Others, You Do To Me

1. This service of reconciliation is suited for a prayer/reflection day for young people.
2. Necessary for the Service: Candles, decoration, posters etc for the central place or places of the ceremony. For the gospel activity, bread, coke, blanket, bandage or medicine, teddy bear or football, book.
3 The selection of hymns depends on the repertoire of the congregation.

WELCOME
All are welcome to our service. We'll listen to the word of God where Jesus says that what we do for others we do for him. We ask his love and forgiveness for all of us:

PRAYER
Lord Jesus, you are our brother, look on us with love; you are the Son of God, look on us with forgiveness; you are the Word of God, look on us with kindness; you are the son of Mary, be with us always, brother and friend. **Amen.**

GOSPEL:
The words of Jesus about helping others is a call and a challenge to examine how we do this in our lives. (This reading may be read, followed by a short drama; or the drama may stand by itself.)

A reading from the gospel according to Matthew:
Jesus said to the people: 'When the Son of man comes in his glory, and all the angels with him, then he will sit on the throne of his glory. All the nations will be gathered before him, and he will separate people one from another as a shepherd separates the sheep from the goats, and he will put

the sheep at his right hand and the goats at the left.
Then the king will say to those at his right hand, 'Come, you that are blessed by my Father, inherit the kingdom prepared for you from the foundation of the world; for I was hungry and you gave me food, I was thirsty and you gave me something to drink, I was a stranger and you welcomed me, I was naked and you gave me clothing, I was sick and you took care of me, I was in prison and you visited me.'
Then the righteous will answer him, 'Lord, when was it that we saw you hungry and gave you food, or thirsty and give you something to drink? And when was it that we saw you a stranger and welcome you, or naked and gave you clothing? And when was it that we saw you sick or in prison and visited you?'
And the king will answer them, 'Truly, I tell you, just as you did it to one of the least of these who are members of my family, you did it to me.'
(Matthew 25:31-40.)

ACTING THE GOSPEL:
8 people in centre representing the 8 needs; 8 more bring to the people in the centre what is needed.

I was hungry and you gave me food – someone brings food to the person in the centre.
I was thirsty and you gave me drink – someone brings water or coke.
I was naked and you clothed me – blanket put around someone.
I was sick and you visited me – someone is bandaged.
I was bullied and you rescued me – person crouches and walks free at another's touch.
I was a stranger and you welcomed me – handshake offered.
I was ignorant and you brought me to school – book given to a person.
I was lonely and you took time with me – teddy bear or football given to a person.

RECONCILIATION SERVICES

REFLECTION ON LIFE:
Have I bullied anyone? **Lord have mercy.**
Have I physically hurt anyone? **Lord have mercy.**
Have I used another just for my own needs or greed? **Lord have mercy.**
Have I neglected to pray or think of God? **Lord have mercy.**
Have I been mean in any way? **Lord have mercy.**
Have I treated people different from myself badly in word or action?
Lord have mercy.

May the God of love and tolerance look kindly on each person here, forgive our wrong-doing and bring us to everlasting life. **Amen.**

VISUAL OF SIN
Each person brings to the centre of the ceremony a symbol of personal or social sin:
A broken bottle for the ways people are violently treated; a torn photo for the destruction of people's creativity; a torn tape or broken mobile phone for the ways we destroy communication among us; some street litter for how we destroy the environment; crushed fruit for how we crush life among us; a broken friendship bracelet for our failures in friendship …

People may go to confession and/or place the symbol at the candle; on their way back they are given a cross as a sign of forgiveness. This cross can be made of stiff paper or pieces of wood. The teacher or priest gives the cross. Some words of Jesus may be written on the cross.

REFLECTION
We like to think that if something went wrong,
we'd get a second chance.
A mistake in a job, a misjudgement in work, a letdown in love,
and we hope we would not be written off for it.
Or things we do that are mean and wrong;
like children stealing something in the kitchen or telling lies –
we'd like another chance.

This is Jesus today –
the one who always sees that a person can change,
do better, act differently the next time.
There's always another chance and a next time with Jesus.
And as he has done for us, he asks us to do for each other.
Even when we've been badly let down.

PRAYER
Lord God,
Lead me from death to life, from falsehood to truth.
Lead me from despair to hope, from fear to trust.
Lead me from hate to love, from war to peace.
Let peace fill our heart, our world, our universe.

BLESSING
May the Lord God bless us with patience with ourselves, so that we can do our best in his service;
May he bless us with patience with others, so we can understand them and be tolerant.
And may we always be blessed with his patience with us,
The Father, Son and Holy Spirit. **Amen.**

HYMN

YOUTH 2

The Unclenched Fist – Opening to Freedom

1. This service of reconciliation is suitable for young people.
2. Necessary for the Service: Candles, decoration, posters etc for the central place or places of the ceremony.
3. The selection of hymns depends on the repertoire of the congregation.

INTRODUCTION

Welcome to our prayer of reconciliation. We want to open our minds and hearts to God, to one another and to love. We want to get rid of what keeps us bitter and harsh, and afraid to do what's best. The image for the prayer service is a clenched fist. We can't receive when our hands are closed. We can also have clenched hearts and forget the goodness of others and of God.

HYMN

PRAYER

Lord Jesus, be among us with forgiveness and with hope. Forgive sins and faults and failings; renew our hope in the goodness of each one here and in your friendship. We make this prayer in the name of Jesus our Lord. **Amen.**

GOSPEL READING

God wants us to live in peace and openness with ourselves and each other. This is the gift of the Holy Spirit.

And he said to them, 'Suppose one of you has a friend, and you go to him at midnight and say to him, 'Friend, lend me three loaves of bread; for a friend of mine has arrived, and I have nothing to set before him.' And he answers from within, 'Do not bother me; the door has already been locked, and my children are with me in bed; I cannot get up and give you anything.' I tell you, even though he will not get up and give him anything because he is his friend, at least because of his persistence he will get up and give him whatever he needs.

So I say to you, Ask, and it will be given you; search, and you will find; knock, and the door will be opened for you. For everyone who asks receives, and everyone who seeks finds, and for everyone who knocks the door will be opened.

Is there one among you, if your child asks for a fish, will give a snake instead of a fish; or if the child asks for an egg, will give a scorpion? If you then, who are evil, know how to give good gifts to your children, how much more will the heavenly Father give the Holy Spirit to those who ask him!'

(Luke 11:5-13.)

ACTIVITY/REFLECTION

Clench your fist and keep it clenched for a short time.
Think of what causes worry and anxiety in your life,
what makes you feel guilty and mean;
you are closed to the air and to any movement of your hand.

Notice your other hand;
it is open, you can move the fingers, you are able to touch gently,
to relax.

Same with our lives.
We can close ourselves to others and to God,
and we are tense, worried, alone.
Our hand cannot console and touch gently when it is clenched.

Notice both hands for a moment or two,
the difference,
and that's something like the difference
between opening and closing to God and others in our lives.

RECONCILIATION SERVICES

EXAMINING MY LIFE:
Christ and goodness
Christ be with me
to give meaning to my life, empty and lonely without him.
We look for meaning in life without God and love, **Lord have mercy.**

Christ before me
to lead me with your light, for you are the Light of the world.
We sometimes follow false or evil guides, **Lord have mercy.**

Christ behind me
to protect me and give me a nudge when I feel like wilting.
We try to go it alone – without God or friends, **Lord have mercy.**

Christ within me
to share my life and keep me true to you.
We neglect God and prayer in life, **Lord have mercy.**

Christ beneath me
to support me in my weakness and when I fall.
We fail to look for the support of God in our lives, **Lord have mercy.**

Christ above me
to be the goal of all my longings and desires.
We place our happiness where we cannot find it, **Lord have mercy.**

Christ at my right hand
to hold me and accompany me on my way, **Lord have mercy.**

Christ on my left hand
to keep me from veering off the road to happiness, **Lord have mercy.**

Christ where I lie
to rest with me and listen to the problems that confront me, **Lord have mercy.**

Christ where I sit
to be my companion as we enjoy each other's company, **Lord have mercy.**

Christ where I arise
to motivate me to keep on serving you in others, **Lord have mercy.**

Christ in the heart of everyone who thinks of me
to unite us together in love.
We judge harshly family and friends, **Lord have mercy.**

Christ in the mouth of all who speak to me
to communicate truthfully God's good news.
We fail to listen to the troubles and worries of other, **Lord have mercy.**

Christ in every eye that sees me
to reveal the wonder and beauty of God's creation, **Lord have mercy.**

Christ in every ear that hears me
To proclaim God's praises and be enraptured with his glory.
We tell lies and gossip about others, **Lord have mercy.**

HYMN

Play some music during individual Confessions
After the confessions:
We pray for the peace of God among ourselves and among everyone:
Lord Jesus Christ, you are the gift of peace to the world.
Give peace of mind and heart to us all here,
make us people of peace and joy among each other;
may we spread the peace of forgiveness when we are hurt,
of tolerance when we can't understand others,
of compassion when others are in trouble.

We offer each other the sign of peace.

RECONCILIATION SERVICES

REFLECTION

Letting Go
There once was a little boy who had a bad temper. His father gave him a bag of nails and told him that every time he lost his temper, he must hammer a nail into the back of the fence. The first day the boy had driven 37 nails into the fence.

Over the next few weeks, as he learned to control his anger, the number of nails hammered daily gradually dwindled down. He discovered it was easier to hold his temper than to drive those nails into the fence …

Finally the day came when the boy didn't lose his temper at all, he told his father about it and the father suggested that the boy now pull out one nail for each day that he was able to hold his temper. The days passed and the young boy was finally able to tell his father that all the nails were gone.

The father took his son by the hand and led him to the fence. He said, 'You have done well my son, but look at the holes in the fence. The fence will never be the same. When you say things in anger, they leave a scar just like this one. You can put a knife in a man and draw it out. It won't matter how many times you say I'm sorry, the wound is still there.'

Please forgive me if I have ever left a hole in your fence.

FINAL PRAYER

Lord God, you are slow to anger and easy to pacify. You have no desire for anyone to die, but that we turn from our evil ways and live. You wait for us until our dying day and readily accept our repentance. You are our creator and know our impulses and that we are but flesh and blood.

We come from dust and end in dust, we win our bread at the risk of our life. We are like the vase that breaks, the grass that withers, the flower that fades, the shadow that passes, the cloud that vanishes, the breeze that blows, the dust that floats, the dream that flies away.

But you are the King, the everlasting God.
God of mercy, hear our prayer, you are Lord forever and ever. **Amen.**

BLESSING

May God, father and mother to all of us, bless us with graces of tolerance and freedom, understanding and forgiveness, all the days of our life.
May God bless all who are near and dear to us,
Father, Son and Holy Spirit, today and every day. **Amen.**

HYMN.

YOUTH 3

Forgiveness – The Light of God

1. This service of reconciliation is suitable for school or a school retreat day.
2. Necessary for the Service: Candles, decoration, posters etc for the central place or places of the ceremony.
3. The selection of hymns depends on the repertoire of the congregation.

HYMN

PRAYER
God of forgiveness and love, you are with us always.
Help us, for our part, to stay close to you.
You have given us the gift of life.
You call us to grow, to develop our talents and to reach our full potential.
You want us to make the world a better place.
May your love and concern for others be made present through us.
We ask this through Christ our Lord. Amen.

READER 1:
St Paul tells how disciples of Jesus and the chosen ones of God should live.

A reading from the letter of St Paul to the Colossians.
As God's chosen ones, holy and beloved, clothe yourselves with compassion, kindness, humility, meekness and patience. Bear with one another and, if anyone has a complaint against another, forgive each other; just as the Lord has forgiven you, so you also must forgive each other. Above all, clothe yourselves with love, which binds everything together in perfect harmony. And let the peace of Christ rule in your hearts, to which indeed you were called in the one body. And be thankful. *(Colossians 3:12-15.)*

(Five students take a candle each and light it from the central candle on the table. They hold the lit candles aloft as they read their prayer below.)

READER 2:

There have been times in my life when I haven't been as good a person as I might have been. I have caused problems at home. I have been quarrelsome and lacking in understanding towards my family. This has caused hurt and was wrong. It destroyed the light of Christ in me.
(Pause. The first smaller candle/light is extinguished.)

READER 3:

There have been times when I haven't made the most of opportunities given to me. I have wasted time. I haven't always used to the full the talents God has given me, particularly in regard to school. I've been lazy. This has been wrong. It destroyed the light of Christ in me.
(Pause. The second smaller candle/light is extinguished.)

READER 4:

There have been times when I've been unfair to my friends and broken my promises. I have talked about them to other friends in a damaging way. Sometimes I have ignored people. I have been choosy. I have been a bad example to my own peer group. This has been wrong. It destroyed the light of Christ in me.
(Pause. The third smaller candle/light is extinguished.)

READER 5:

There have been times, God, when I have neglected my relationship with you. I have not prayed or have been very careless when praying. I have been giddy at Mass or even missed it altogether. This has been wrong. It destroyed the light of Christ in me.
(Pause. The fourth smaller candle/light is extinguished.)

READER 6:

There have been times when I've been dishonest with people around me. I've told lies because I hadn't the courage to own up. I haven't always respected others or their belongings. I've been slow in returning things I've borrowed. This has been wrong. It destroyed the light of Christ in me.
(Pause. The fifth smaller candle/light is extinguished.)

RECONCILIATION SERVICES

LEADER:

Sometimes we have blown out the light of Christ in our own lives. We recall now the ways in which we may have done so over the past year.
- Have you been helpful at home? Do you always do what you are asked? Or do you moan and try to get out of helping?
- Have you lost your temper at home? Maybe you shouted at someone, or slammed a door, or refused to talk?
- Have you always remembered the way God sees you? Have you treated your home as special? Have you failed to treat the people with whom you live with kindness, understanding and compassion?
- Are you always honest? Or have you lied to someone? What is your attitude to so-called 'little white lies'?
- Are you a good friend? Have you hurt one of your friends? Have you been unkind because you were hurt or annoyed?
- Are you kind to the other students in our class? Have you hurt someone's feelings this year? Have you made it difficult for others to get to know you?

We pause now and take some time to look at our lives, to be more sensitive to what our conscience says. *(Pause.)*

HYMN

Together now, we acknowledge our failures to live the Christian message of love, as we say:
I confess to almighty God ...

READER 2:

Lord, I promise to be a better person at home, making a special effort to love and respect my family, thereby bringing your light into our world. *(Pause. The first smaller candle/light is relit.)*

READER 3:

Lord, I promise, with your help, to respect life more, especially my own. I will use my talents more fully in the future for your service and for the service of others, thereby spreading your light in the world.
(Pause. The second smaller candle/light is relit.)

READER 4:

Lord, I will be a better friend in the future. I will try to be more loyal and caring. I will be careful not to belittle people by talking about them to others. In this way I will spread your light in our world.
(Pause. The third smaller candle/light is relit.)

READER 5:

Lord, in the future, with your help, I will try to be a better person. I will stay close to you in prayer and will be more attentive at Mass. In this way I will spread your light in our world.
(Pause. The fourth smaller candle/light is relit.)

READER 6:

Lord, I will try to be more honest. I will respect others and their belongings. I will tell the truth. In this way I will spread your light in our world.
(Pause. The fifth smaller candle/light is relit.)

LEADER:

Loving God, source of our life, you know our weaknesses. May we reach out with joy to grasp your hand and walk more readily in our ways. We ask this through Christ our Lord.

ALL: **Amen**.

HYMN

ON RETREAT

Be healed, be strong, be forgiven

1. This service of reconciliation is for a day of recollection or retreat, when people have been together in a prayerful situation for some time.
2. Necessary for the Service: Candles, decoration, posters etc for the central place or places of the ceremony. Pieces of paper, pen/pencils, ribbon. A cross in the sanctuary or central area.
3. The selection of hymns depends on the repertoire of the congregation.

INTRODUCTION

Prayer can make us receptive to the love and the forgiveness of God, and also to the needs we have to receive the strength, forgiveness and healing graces of God in our lives.
The sacrament of reconciliation celebrates our healing, our strength and our forgiveness. We bring our past with its baggage of wounds and sin to God, and our hope to live in his love and the spirit of his love for the future. We begin this service of reconciliation with a hymn and then our prayers for strength, healing and forgiveness.

HYMN

PRAYER

Good and gracious God, strong and living, give us the strength and courage to live in the spirit of your gospel; give us also your healing grace so that we live in the freedom of your children, and heal us of what blocks the flow and growth of love within us. You are the God of life, of love and of a new beginning. Begin new life each day within us, begin new love of you and others, begin again the joy of our birth when we were born in your love. Open us, good and gracious God, to receive your love and human love in the depths of our personality. We ask this through Christ our Lord. Amen.

The word of God from the prophet Isaiah.
The past need not be remembered in the presence of God. Once forgiven, it is now held forever in forgiveness.

Thus says the Lord,
who makes a way in the sea,
a path in the mighty waters,
'Remember not the former things,
nor consider the things of old.
Behold, I am doing a new thing;
now it springs forth, do you not perceive it?
I will make a way in the wilderness
and rivers in the desert.
The wild beasts will honour me,
the jackals and the ostriches;
for I give water in the wilderness,
rivers in the desert,
to give drink to my chosen people,
The people whom I formed for myself
that they might declare my praise.'
(Isaiah 43:16-21)

Or

A Reading from the prophet Ezekiel.
The hard heart is softened in the forgiveness and strength of God.
For I will take you from the nations, and gather you from all the countries, and bring you into your own land. I will sprinkle clean water upon you, and you shall be clean from all your uncleannesses, and from all your idols I will cleanse you. A new heart I will give you, and a new spirit I will put within you; and I will remove from your body the heart of stone and give you a heart of flesh. And I will put my spirit within you, and make you follow my statutes and be careful to observe my ordinances. Then you shall live in the land that I gave to your ancestors; and you shall be my people, and I will be your God.
(Ezekiel 36:24-28)

RECONCILIATION SERVICES

Or

A Reading from the Book of Sirach.
We are strengthened in our freedom to choose to follow the way of God. If you choose, you can keep the commandments.
Do not say, 'It was the Lord's doing that I fell away';
for he does not do what he hates.
Do not say, 'It was he who led me astray';
for he had no need of the sinful.
The Lord hates all abominations,
such things are not loved by those who fear him.
It was he who created humankind in the beginning,
and he left them in the power of their own free choice.
If you choose, you can keep the commandments,
and to act faithfully is a matter of your own choice.
He has placed before you fire and water:
stretch out your hand for whichever you wish.
Before each person are life and death,
and whichever one chooses will be given.
For great is the wisdom of the Lord;
he is mighty in power and sees everything;
his eyes are on those who fear him,
and he knows every human action.
He has not commanded anyone to be wicked,
and he has not given anyone permission to sin.
(Sirach 15:11-20)

HYMN

GOSPEL
The gospel story invites us to ask the Lord for what we really want in our lives in this prayer of reconciliation.

As he approached Jericho, a blind man was sitting by the roadside begging. When he heard a crowd going by, he asked what was happening. They told him, 'Jesus of Nazareth is passing by.' Then he shouted, 'Jesus, Son of David, have mercy on me!' Those who were in front sternly ordered him to be quiet; but he shouted even more loudly, 'Son of David, have mercy on me!' Jesus stood still and ordered the man to be brought to him; and when he came near, he asked him, 'What do you want me to do for you?' He said, 'Lord, let me see again.' Jesus said to him, 'Receive your sight; your faith has saved you.' Immediately he regained his sight and followed him, glorifying God; and all the people, when they saw it, praised God.
(Luke 18:35-43)

RITUAL
People are invited to write on a small piece of paper their need for forgiveness, or healing or strength in their lives: sins or events of the past or weaknesses in the present, or just aspects of personality which block receptivity to God's love. After some time they are invited to place these pieces of paper on the cross (the written side on the wooden side so that the writing is private).

While people move to the sanctuary, a hymn may be sung, or suitable music be played.

On their return from the sanctuary or from individual confession, a ribbon of forgiveness and healing is placed on them.

SCRIPTURE REFLECTION:
Clothed in colour and glory.
I will greatly rejoice in the Lord,
my soul shall exult in my God;
for he has clothed me with the garments of salvation,
he has covered me with the robe of righteousness,
as a bridegroom decks himself with a garland,
and as a bride adorns herself with her jewels.

RECONCILIATION SERVICES

For as the earth brings forth its shoots,
and as a garden causes what is sown in it to spring up,
so the Lord God will cause righteousness and praise
to spring forth before all the nations.
(Isaiah 61:10-11)

PRAYER

Let us pray as Jesus taught us for the capacity to forgive others:
Our Father ...
Prayer for peace and reconciliation in the world:
Lord Jesus Christ, you said to your apostles ...

FINAL PRAYER

Father, those who work for peace are called your children. May we never tire of praying and working for peace in our world that is based on justice and does justice. May we know always in our lives your healing strength, courage and love. We make this prayer through Christ our Lord. **Amen.**

BLESSING

May God the Father bless us with strength; may the Son of Mary bless us with healing and the Spirit of both bless us with forgiveness.

May the strength of the Father empower us to live by the gospel; may the healing of the Son enliven our hearts and bodies with the energy of the gospel, and may the forgiveness of the Spirit flow from us to others.

And may God bless us, Father of strength, Son of our healing and Spirit of forgiveness, now and every day, **Amen.**

HYMN

FOR GENERAL USE

Call to Justice

1. This service of reconciliation is for general use or for a workshop/reflection day on justice.
2. Necessary for the Service: Candles, decoration, posters etc for the central place or places of the ceremony. Leaves from a tree.
3. The selection of hymns depends on the repertoire of the congregation.

HYMN

PRAYER AND INTRODUCTION

Our service focuses on the sin of the world. We are not personally to blame for poverty, starvation and the greed of the world. But it is the neglect and sin of the human race which causes such suffering. We pray God's mercy on the world, and the conversion of hearts so that all may enjoy the fruits of the earth. We are not to blame, but we can be part of the solution.

And we pray:
Lord, what is the point of your presence if our lives do not alter?
Change our lives, shatter our complacency.
Take away that self-regard which makes our consciences feel clear.
Press us uncomfortably.
Make of our hearts your heart.
For only thus will peace and justice be made,
your justice and peace.
We make this prayer through Christ our Lord.
Amen.

RECONCILIATION SERVICES

READING:
God's word challenges us to conversion: it tells us that he is pleased with works of justice, not just hymns and prayers.

Reading from the Prophet Amos:
The Lord says: 'I hate, I despise your festivals,
and I take no delight in your solemn assemblies.
Even though you offer me your burnt offerings and grain offerings,
I will not accept them,
and the offerings of well-being of your fatted animals
I will not look upon.
Take away from me the noise of your songs;
I will not listen to the melody of your harps.
But let justice roll down like waters,
and righteousness like an ever-flowing stream.
(Amos 5:21-24)

Or

Reading from the Book of Sirach:
A call to care for the poor.

My child, do not cheat the poor of their living,
and do not keep needy eyes waiting.
Do not grieve the hungry,
or anger one in need.
Do not add to the troubles of the desperate,
nor delay giving to the needy.
Do not reject a suppliant in distress,
nor turn your face away from the poor.
Do not avert your eye from the needy,
and give no one reason to curse you;
for if in bitterness of soul some should curse you,
their Creator will hear their prayer.

ON JUSTICE

Endear yourself to the congregation;
bow your head low to the great.
Give a hearing to the poor,
and return their greeting politely.
Rescue the oppressed from the oppressor;
and do not be hesitant in giving a verdict.
Be a father to orphans,
and like a husband to their mother;
you will then be like a son of the Most High,
and he will love you more than does your mother.
(Sirach 4:1-10)

REFLECTION
A call to stand with people, and thus with God.

I know you as my God and stand apart –
I do not know you as my own and come closer.
I stand not where you come down and own yourself as mine,
there to clasp you to my heart and take you as my comrade.
You are the Brother among brothers,
but I heed them not.
I divide not my earnings with them,
thus sharing my all with you.
In pleasure and pain I stand not by the side of men,
and thus stand by you.
I shrink to give up my life
and thus do not plunge into the great waters of life.
Tagore.

GOSPEL
This story from Jesus highlights inequality and injustice in the world, and challenges us to be proactive in our response. Dives' sin was that he did nothing.

RECONCILIATION SERVICES

Reading from the Gospel of Luke.
Jesus spoke this parable to his disciples: 'There was a rich man, who was dressed in purple and fine linen and who feasted sumptuously every day. And at his gate lay a poor man named Lazarus, covered with sores, who longed to satisfy his hunger with what fell from the rich man's table; even the dogs would come and licked his sores. The poor man died and was carried away by the angels to be with Abraham. The rich man also died and was buried. In Hades, where he was being tormented, he looked up and saw Abraham far away with Lazarus by his side. He called out, 'Father Abraham, have mercy on me, and send Lazarus to dip the tip of his finger in water and cool my tongue; for I am in agony in these flames.' But Abraham said, 'Child, remember that during your lifetime you received your good things, and Lazarus in like manner evil things; but now he is comforted here, and you are in agony. And besides all this, between you and us a great chasm has been fixed, so that those who might want to pass from here to you cannot do so, and no one can cross from there to us.' He said, 'Then, father, I beg you to send him to my father's house – for I have five brothers – that he may warn them, so that they will not also come into this place of torment.' But Abraham said, 'They have Moses and the prophets; they should listen to them.' He said, 'No, father Abraham; but if some one goes to them from the dead, they will repent.' He said to him, 'If they do not listen to Moses and the prophets, neither will they be convinced even if someone rises from the dead.'
(Luke 16:19-31)

PRAYER FOR MERCY
We pray the mercy of God and his forgiveness on our world:
For starvation, homelessness and famine, we pray to the Lord of generosity,
Lord have mercy.
For violence, war and bitterness, we pray to the Lord of peace,
Christ have mercy.
For inequality, murder and theft, we pray to the Lord of kindness,
Lord have mercy.

May the God of hope and justice have mercy on us:
For failure to notice inequality and poverty, **Lord have mercy.**
For neglect of the poor and the needy, **Christ have mercy.**
For silence in the face of others' needs, **Lord have mercy.**

May the God of compassion and kindness have mercy on us:
Lord you love justice and you love the poor, **Lord have mercy.**
Lord you want peace and walk with people of peace, **Christ have mercy.**
Lord you want joy and love for all your people, **Lord have mercy.**

May the God of peace and truth have mercy on us, forgive us our sins, and bring us today and forever to everlasting life. Amen.

RITUAL OF LEAVES
As people return from confession, or from a place of prayer in the sanctuary, they are given a branch of a tree – the branch of justice. Let this branch invite them to pray and work for justice. The branch of a tree reminds us that we are part of the tree of God: we are branches, Jesus is the vine, the life and the trunk of the tree.

REFLECTION
We hold our leaves and reflect on the word of God:

I am the vine, you are the branches.
I am the stem, you are the leaves.
I am the root, you are the flowers.

I am the rose, you are the fragrance.
I am the wheat, you are the bread.
I am the vine, you are the grapes.

I am the life, the truth and the way;
You are the energy, the question and the sign.
Without you my word cannot be heard,
My bread cannot be broken
and my life cannot be shared.

You are my justice, peace and joy in the world.

RECONCILIATION SERVICES

Glory be to the Father, and to the Son and to the Holy Spirit;
as it was in the beginning, is now and ever shall be,
world without end. **Amen.**

FINAL SCRIPTURE
Sow for yourselves righteousness,
reap steadfast love;
break up your fallow ground,
for it is time to seek the Lord,
that he may come and rain righteousness upon you.
(Hosea 10:12)

PRAYER
Circle us Lord with your love,
embrace us with your presence,
enliven us with your joy.
Keep darkness out, keep light within.
Keep fear without, keep peace within.
Keep guilt without, keep forgiveness within.
Keep shame without, keep acceptance within.
Keep bitterness without, keep compassion within.
Keep us in love, strengthen us in love,
call us in love today and everyday. **Amen.**

BLESSING
Cease to do evil, learn to do good; search for justice, help the oppressed and the poor; the starving, the elderly, the lonely, the imprisoned.
Be just to the orphan, the single parent, the mentally and physically disabled. Plead for the widow, the refugee and the immigrant.
Go in peace to love and serve the Lord and his people.

HYMN

FOR MARRIED COUPLES

Our Love may Grow

1. This service of reconciliation is for a prayer/reflection day for married couples. Note that the prayers and rituals presume that the participants are couples. In situations where not all are couples, it will need adaptation.
2. Necessary for the Service: Candles, decoration, posters etc for the central place or places of the ceremony. A candle should be placed near each of the participants who assist at the exchange of rings during the service. Thus, each should have their wedding ring. A small candle for each person.
3. The selection of hymns depends on the repertoire of the congregation.

HYMN

PRAYER
Over the years, you have brought us together in the sacrament of marriage; your presence has embraced us at all times, and will continue to do so. Give us, Lord God, the mind of Jesus that we may think like him and the heart of Jesus that we may love like him. Help us enjoy the personality of the other, accept our differences and rejoice in them, and be truly grateful for our love.

INTRODUCTION
We gather as two communities: the community of the couple and the community of the couples here. We pray for the growth of love and enjoyment of each other in our marriages.
We gather as people who have at times let each other down, have deliberately or unwittingly hurt each other; we gather in the grace of the sacrament of marriage, knowing that God is present in our love, and that his love invites and empowers us to put away the effects of selfishness, faults and failings, and promise love in the future with joy and courage.

RECONCILIATION SERVICES

We gather into the present: that God is love and we are love to each other. That love and only love is the root of our commitment and the source of our joy.

PRAYER TOGETHER

For the times of selfishness when a little compromise might have gone a long way, **Lord have mercy.**
For failures to listen, **Lord have mercy.**
For failure to take into account the other's shortcomings, **Lord have mercy.**
For neglect of God in our marriage, **Lord have mercy.**
For giving time to other good tasks but to the neglect of our relationship, **Lord have mercy.**
For failures to say thanks and sorry, **Lord have mercy.**

(and other petitions)

Let us pray: May the God of goodness and love look kindly on our faults, help us in our struggles and remind us always that in the love we give and share, we find his presence close to us always, now and forever. **Amen.**

PSALM

We pray the psalm together:

Turn your ear O Lord and give answer
for I am poor and needy.
Preserve my life for I am faithful,
save the servant who trusts in you.

You are my God, have mercy on me Lord,
for I cry to you all the day long.
Give joy to your servant, O Lord,
for to you I lift up my soul.

O Lord, you are good and forgiving,
full of love to all who call.

Give heed, O Lord, to my prayer,
and attend to the sound of my voice.
(from Psalm 85)

GOSPEL

Growth happens all the time – whether we plan it or not. The same in marriage as in the earth: God grows each and the couple.

And he said, 'The kingdom of God is as if someone would scatter seed on the ground, and would sleep and rise night and day, and the seed would sprout and grow, he does not know how. The earth produces of itself, first the stalk, then the head, then the full grain in the head. But when the grain is ripe, at once he goes in with his sickle, because the harvest has come.'
(Mark 4:26-29)

Or

In marriage we are strength to each other, like salt for food and light in darkness.

Jesus said to the disciples: 'You are the salt of the earth; but if salt has lost its taste, how can its saltiness be restored? It is no longer good for anything, but is thrown out and trampled under foot.
'You are the light of the world. A city set on a hill cannot be hid. No one after lighting a lamp puts it under a bushel basket, but on the lampstand, and it gives light to all in the house. In the same way, let your light shine before others, so that they may see your good works and give glory to your Father in heaven.
(Matthew 5:13-17)

RECONCILIATION SERVICES

RITUAL

Together couples come to one of the prayer-leaders of this ceremony, and pray a blessing on their wedding rings:
Lord, God of faithful love,
bless the circle of our love with the grace of your life;
bless what has been broken with your healing,
bless our future which we look to in trust,
trust of you and trust in each other,
through Christ our Lord. Amen.

Exchange of rings, as in the marriage ceremony:

Couple say as in the marriage ceremony, putting the ring on each other's finger:
…, I give you this ring as a sign of our faithful love, in the name of the Father, and of the son and of the Holy Spirit.

Then each places his or her left hand over a candle, receiving the love of God onto the circle of his/her wedding love and ring.
As they do this, they pray for the other.

Opportunity for private confession at this time, during which music may be played or hymns be sung. At this point there is also an invitation for couples to ask for forgiveness from each other if they so wish.

PRAYER OF THANKS
Preface 1 of the Marriage Rite.

HYMN

PRAYER FOR PEACE
For peace of mind and heart for all here,
Lord hear our prayer.
For peace and comfort for those whose spouse has died,
Lord hear our prayer.
For peace and courage for those whose spouses are ill,
Lord hear our prayer.
For peace and hope for those who have separated or divorced,
Lord hear our prayer.

FOR MARRIED COUPLES

For peace and trust for those whose are experiencing difficulties in their marriages,
Lord hear our prayer.
For peace and joy in our family life.
Lord hear our prayer.

SIGN OF PEACE

REFLECTION

Love exists because God exists,
and God is alive when love is alive.
Look no farther for the love of God
than to the love you promise to each other.
Look no farther for the birth of God
than to the love you have brought to birth in each other.
Look no farther for the faithfulness of God
than to the 'yes' you have said to each other.

Love is God one to another
and your God is near to you in love.

Or

Now we feel no rain, for each of us will be a shelter to the others.
Now we feel no cold, for each of us will be warmth to the other.
Now there is no aloneness, for each of us will be a companion to the other.

We are two bodies, but there is one life between us and one home.
When evening falls I will look up and you will be there.
I'll take your hand; you'll take mine
and we'll turn together
to look at the road we travelled to reach this place
and the hour of our happiness.

RECONCILIATION SERVICES

It stretches behind us, even as the future lies ahead.
A long and winding road, and every turning means discovery.
Old hopes, new laughter, shared fears.
The adventure has just begun.
(American Indian Wedding Blessing.)

BLESSINGS
Each couple turns to the couple beside them and blesses them:

May you find the blessing of God in the love of your marriage;
may you find the love of your marriage enhanced by the friends you make and the community of the church,
embracing always the God who embraces you,
Father, Son and Holy Spirit.

The couple then bless each other:
Thanking you for your love, I give you God's blessing;
trusting in your love, I pray God's blessing for you,
sharing our love, I pray God's blessing on all we love,
Father, Son and Holy Spirit. **Amen.**

FINAL BLESSING
Receive the candle of married love, and be blessed with the faithful light of God, and in receiving this candle, commit yourselves to love of each other, of your family and all you meet.
And may God bless you now and always, Father, Son and Holy Spirit.
Amen.

HYMN